THEN AND THERE SERIES
GENERAL EDITOR
MARJORIE REEVES

G000254630

The Chartists in Wales

PETER SEARBY

Illustrated from contemporary sources

LONGMAN

LONGMAN GROUP UK LIMITED
*Longman House, Burnt Mill, Harlow, Essex CM20 2JE, UK
and Associated Companies throughout the World.*

First published 1986
ISBN 0 582 22172 2

*Set in 11/12½ pt Baskerville, Linotron 202
Produced by Longman Group (F.E.) Limited
Printed in Hong Kong*

Contents

To the Reader

In July 1981 an unemployed man in Liverpool was asked on TV what was so unpleasant about being out of work. He spoke of being poor and feeling that the weeks were empty, and added that the worst thing was that 'you feel that other people are running your life. You have no control over it.'

This book is about people who lived in Wales 150 years ago. They too often felt that they had no control over their own lives, and they tried to get it by fighting for the *'People's Charter'* – a list of powers and rights they drew up and claimed for ordinary people.

When they had jobs, their lives were hard and their employers harsh. Often they had no work, and then they were pushed around by the *Poor Law*, which was supposed to look after them but instead treated them brutally. So they were not only poor; they were also made to feel that being poor was a crime.

Today, we can try to improve our lives by using our votes to elect MPs we like, so that they will work in Parliament for us. The people in this book had no votes. Getting votes for ordinary men (though not women) was the chief aim of the Charter. But behind it was the wish to use this new power to make their everyday lives happier. One man said that the Charter meant 'better wages, limited hours of labour, comfort, independence, happiness – all that the fond heart of suffering man pictures to himself of joy and prosperity in his happiest moments'.

This book is about *Chartists* in Wales. But there were Chartists all over Britain. They had a newspaper, the 'Northern Star', which was read by Chartists everywhere from Pembroke to Aberdeen. They planned their actions together, and Chartists from Wales and Scotland often went to London for meetings. The most famous Chartist in Wales, John Frost, was a hero all over Britain.

Prices were very much lower in Chartist times than they are today. Usually £1 would buy what £30 would buy today. This means that you have to multiply sums of money by thirty to get their value today. Of course, wages were much lower too.

In the 1830s and 1840s a four-pound (2 kg) loaf usually cost between 5*d*. and 7*d*. (2p and 3p), butter about 1*s*. 6*d*. (7½p) a pound (453 g), cheap tea 4*s*. (20p) a pound, and potatoes 3*s*. (15p) a hundredweight (50 kg). A five-room house could be rented for 4*s*. (20p) a week. On the other hand some workers earned as little as 5*s*. (25p) a week. For them the time described in this book was the 'Hungry Forties'.

England and Wales in Chartist times, showing places mentioned in this book

1 Living in Wales in the 1800s

MINERS AND IRONWORKERS IN SOUTH WALES

In 1750 South Wales was a land of farms and villages. Then coalmining and ironmaking began in the valleys. To work in the new industries men moved from nearby farms, and sometimes from as far away as Hereford and Gloucester over the border. Towns grew very quickly, spreading like dirty ribbons along the steep valleys. Close-packed terraces climbed up the hills on either side. Coal tips loomed up at the back, and at the front coal waggons rattled along *tramroads* to the ironworks.

Coalmining was far more dangerous than today. Roofs collapsed, mines flooded, and gas caused explosions. Mineowners did not seem to care about the many deaths in their mines. This helped to make the miners dislike them.

Miners and ironworkers were paid high wages when their industries were booming, or doing well, and profits were large; for example, in 1839 miners earned about 27s. (£1.35) a week and ironworkers about 35s. (£1.75). These were much higher earnings than farmworkers' – about 9s. (45p). (Remember to multiply these amounts by about 30 to get their value today.) But very often *booms* were ended by *slumps* when wages were slashed and thousands lost their jobs. For example, wages sank by 1844 to 13s. (65p) for miners and 24s. (£1.20) for ironworkers.

Often workers were paid in coins which could only be used in shops owned by their employers. These were called 'truck' shops. Quality was poor and prices high. But there was very little that workers could do about it. One man said in 1841

that in the village of Blackwood, because of the company shop 'there is a terrorism existing over the men, and they dare not speak out'. It is not surprising that Blackwood became a centre of Chartism.

Workers sometimes went on strike, but usually without getting what they wanted. Trade unions did not have much money to support workers on strike so strikes could not last long. Employers brought in *blacklegs* to fill the jobs of the strikers. If strikers gathered in crowds, soldiers were used to chase them away. Strike leaders were sacked.

Between 1820 and 1835 miners and ironworkers sometimes used violence to try to get what they wanted. In the evening after work they gathered on the hillsides, blacking their faces and wearing masks as disguises to keep themselves safe from capture. They were called the 'Scotch Cattle', probably because they reminded people of black-faced bulls. They visited blacklegs and employers in the middle of the night in parties of ten or twenty, spreading fear by rattling chains as they drew near to the victims' houses. Blacklegs were beaten up, and their furniture and clothing burned. In 1832 one blackleg wrote to his employer that he was 'a feard of my life in til you will pleas to settel some way or a Nother with the men that we may work with peace'. The Scotch Cattle made people used to violence in parts of South Wales; it helps to explain why some Chartists were willing to use violence too.

THE FLANNEL WEAVERS OF POWYS

Another part of Wales where people were poor and unhappy, and where there were many Chartists, was the old county of Montgomeryshire. This is now part of Powys. In the towns of Llanidloes and Newtown there were about 1500 weavers making flannel (a warm woollen cloth) on handlooms. As their name shows, handlooms were worked not by steam, or water power, but human muscles – though in fact feet were

Opposite: A coalmine near Aberdare in 1852, shortly after Chartist times. Notice the canal, bridges, boats carrying coal, and winding-gear worked by a horse

as much in use as hands. Looms were in workshops, each of which usually had ten or more looms; often the 'loomshops' were on the top floor of a four-storey building.

Weavers' lives were hard. Even when there was plenty of work men were only paid between 7s. (35p) and 11s. (55p) a week for 14 hours' work a day. Women and children were paid a lot less, and their labour made it possible for the masters to keep down the men's wages. There was usually a lot of work in the summer, when shops were building up their stocks of flannel for the winter trade. But in the winter shops were buying lighter cloth for the summer, and the flannel weavers had little work. 'A slight *depression* in the trade throws men out of work', said one government inquiry. Booms and slumps hit the flannel industry constantly; life was like being on a switchback.

Weavers often went on strike against their low wages and tough lives – once for as long as eight weeks. But there were more weavers than work and masters were not worried by a strike. So it is not surprising that like the miners and iron-workers further south the weavers of mid-Wales turned to the People's Charter.

CAN PARLIAMENT HELP?

Very few British people had votes and could help to elect Members of Parliament. No women did, and some Chartists called for votes for them, as well as for men. In 1830 only about 10 per cent of Welsh men over 21 had votes either, and those who had them were mostly richer people – landowners, factory owners, shopkeepers, and lawyers. Working people thought their chance was coming with the Reform Bill of 1832, in which the *Whig* government promised to give votes to more people. More shopkeepers and farmers got the vote, and the number of voters in Wales was doubled with about 20 per cent of men now voting.

Opposite: Flannel weavers' cottages at Llanidloes, built about 1820. The looms were on the top floor

But in the end most working men all over Britain found that they still did not have the vote. Working people felt that the Whigs had cheated them: 'those very men from whom we expected so much, and who have promised so much, only to deceive', as one Chartist put it. This was why Chartists disliked equally the two big political parties of the day. *Tories* and Whigs quarrelled with each other, but neither of them were friends of working people.

After the 1832 Reform Bill, too, there were other ways in which it was hard for ordinary people to have power in Parliament. MPs had to own a certain amount of property, and they were not paid. So it was impossible for people like miners and ironworkers to be MPs. Also, electors voted openly by naming in a loud voice the man they chose. There was no secret *ballot*, as today. So it was easy to bribe electors to vote in a particular way, and also to sack them if they didn't choose the man their employers wanted. These things often happened.

Another complaint of ordinary people was that general elections were held only every seven years. Public opinion might change in that time, and people might want to change their MP. *Constituencies* were also very unequal in size; some were very big, others tiny. So in one place 500 men would elect an MP, and in another 10,000.

Chartists complained about all these matters and in the People's Charter demanded changes, as you can read in Chapter 2.

STAMPING OUT POVERTY–BY STAMPING ON THE POOR

In each parish in England and Wales poor people – the unemployed, sick and very old – were kept from starving by payments of a few shillings a week. This money was called 'poor relief', and it was collected by charging rates on the value of all houses and land in the parish. If a ratepayer had a house worth £30 a year and the rate was 10*s*. (50p) in the pound, he would have to pay £15 a year in poor rates.

Poor rates went up and down with slumps and booms, but

in the 1820s they averaged over £6,000,000 a year. Rate-payers, most of them better-off than Welsh ironworkers, thought they were paying too much. The Whig government agreed with them, and in 1834 pushed through Parliament the Poor Law Amendment Act in an attempt to lower the rates which property owners paid. In future unemployed people who wanted poor relief had to go into a *workhouse* to get it. Workhouses were to be grim and unwelcoming places, so that the unemployed would take any job rather than enter one and spend the ratepayers' money.

The act certainly cut the amount spent on poor relief, by about one fifth. It also enraged working people throughout Britain. The new workhouses were bleak, and painted in dark colours. The food was deliberately made dull to discourage the poor from entering the workhouse. At Carmarthen work-house the poor were fed on black barley bread, potatoes and soup, with 1½ oz (40 g) of cheese on Mondays and Thurs-days and 3½ oz (100 g) of meat on Sundays and Wednesdays. On Fridays they were given one herring each. The food in the local gaol was better.

Under the new act *paupers* outside the workhouse were often very badly treated too. One case which became very well known in Wales was that of William Thomas, an invalid living with his two sons near Carmarthen. His cottage was a ruin. They had no bed-clothes. The local poor law *guardians* refused to pay him more than 3s. (15p) a week, saying that any extra should be earned by his sons. He died of starvation in November 1843.

Poor law officials in Wales were sometimes attacked by angry people, and had to be escorted by soldiers. Fear of what might happen stopped poor law guardians from building workhouses in many places in Wales. Even before the Narberth workhouse was finished someone tried to burn it down, in January 1839. The biggest attack was on Carmarthen workhouse in June 1843. Over 2,000 men marched through the town, one of them carrying a placard saying 'Cyfiawnder a charwyr cyfiawnder ydyn ni oll'

(Justice, and lovers of justice are we all). When they reached the workhouse they frightened the master into giving up his keys. The mob then let themselves in; they smashed furniture up and threw the bedding out of the windows, while one pauper woman danced on a table with glee. Then the cavalry arrived. Hearing that there was going to be trouble, they had galloped towards Carmarthen so fast that one horse dropped dead. But the cavalry scattered the rioters, who ran away through the streets of the town.

Six years before the attack on Carmarthen workhouse *Radicals* all over Britain grouped together to fight poverty and the harsh new Poor Law. They were fighting for the People's Charter.

Opposite: Inside a workhouse in 1843 – the room for women. Notice the beds, and the women gathered round the stove

2 The Birth of the Charter

THE DEMANDS OF THE PEOPLE

By 1837 ordinary British people were feeling that they needed the power to elect MPs who would make Parliament pass laws which would help them. Radicals in London drew up a list of what they wanted. They thought of six demands; often they were called the Six Points. They were also called the People's Charter – a name that had often been given to demands for rights since the Great Charter (Magna Carta) of 1215.

The Six Points of the Charter were:

1. A VOTE for every man over twenty-one, who was not insane or in prison. This demand was sometimes called MANHOOD SUFFRAGE. Some Chartists wanted votes for women too.

2. The SECRET BALLOT. This was to make it possible for people to give their votes without fear of what might happen to them.

3. NO PROPERTY QUALIFICATION for members of Parliament, that is, an end to the rule that MPs must own land. This was to make it possible for poor men to become MPs.

4. PAYMENT OF MEMBERS OF THE HOUSE OF COMMONS. Without payment poor men could not afford to become MPs.

5. EQUAL CONSTITUENCIES, so that places of the same size had the same number of MPs and therefore the same amount of power.

6. ANNUAL PARLIAMENTS. In the 1830s there were usually seven years between elections. Annual elections would mean that if people in the country changed their minds, the govern-

ment and its plans could change too. They would also make it harder for men to buy their way into Parliament by bribing electors. Bribery every year would be expensive.

An idea of putting the Six Points to Parliament in a petition, or request, came from Birmingham. A newspaper editor there wrote of a 'petition signed by two million men, drawn, like a Cheshire cheese of twenty feet diameter, in a cart of white horses to the House of Commons'. You can see a picture of a petition being taken to Parliament on page 45. The two ideas were put together, and the Charter was presented to Parliament several times in petitions, as we shall see.

CHARTIST CLUBS IN WALES

By the end of 1838 there were Chartists in most parts of England, Scotland and Wales. In Wales most Chartists lived in the towns in the south where coal was mined and iron made, towns like Merthyr and Blackwood (see the map on p. 36). There were also Chartists in other Welsh towns and some in the countryside too. But more farmers were 'Rebeccaites' than Chartists. You can read about the way the followers of 'Rebecca' showed their anger in another Then and There book called 'The Rebecca Riots'.

Chartists formed clubs and held regular meetings, perhaps three or four times a week. They often met in public houses, which had rooms big enough to hold them. Meetings were fun. In days when there were no cinemas, radio or TV people enjoyed talking and arguing very much. Chartists often sang, or listened to people reciting poems. Sometimes they listened while someone read a Chartist newspaper like the 'Northern Star'. This was published in Leeds, and read all over Britain. It cost $4\frac{1}{2}d$. (2p) and was too expensive for all Chartists to buy their own copy. Besides, not all Chartists could read.

At their meetings Chartists drank beer, which was why *publicans* allowed them to hold their meetings in their houses. But many Welsh Chartists disliked alcohol and urged people to stop drinking it, saying that it was a waste of money and 17

THE NORTHERN STAR AND LEEDS GENERAL ADVERTISER.

VOL. II. No. 62. SATURDAY, JANUARY 19, 1839. PRICE FOURPENCE HALFPENNY, or Five Shillings per Quarter.

NATIONAL RENT. NATIONAL PETITION. GENERAL CONVENTION.

RADICAL REFORMERS,

THE NATIONAL PETITION MUST BE COMPLETED BY THE TWENTY-THIRD DAY OF JANUARY.

THE LANCASHIRE and CHESHIRE PETITIONS must be forwarded (Carriage Free) to R. J. RICHARDSON, Bookseller, 19, Chapel-Street, Salford, on or before the above Date.

The YORKSHIRE PETITIONS must be forwarded (Carriage Free) to the *Northern Star* Office, Leeds.

The NORTHUMBERLAND and DURHAM PETITIONS must be forwarded (Carriage Free) to the *Northern Liberator* Office, Newcastle-upon-Tyne.

The CUMBERLAND and WESTMORELAND PETITIONS must be forwarded (Carriage Free) to Mr. ARTHUR, Rickergate, Carlisle.

NO TIME MUST BE LOST.

THE GENERAL CONVENTION WILL MEET ON THE FOURTH OF FEB. NEXT.

EDWARD NIGHTINGALE, Chairman.

Manchester, January 11th, 1839.

CHALLENGE TO CURE BLINDNESS.

MR. BAXTER, from Hull, (please to observe the name) who has performed such extraordinary Cures on persons, many of whom have been blind for five, ten, fifteen, twenty, thirty, and forty-five years, begs to announce to the Public, that he has permanently taken up his Residence in Leeds, and will pledge himself to cure all external Diseases of the Eye, Dimness of Sight, &c., without blisters, bleeding, seton, issues, or any restraint of Diet.

Cataracts I cannot cure, as I make no use of an instrument to any Eye. In cases of Amaurosis, I can tell if there be any hopes after the first Application I make to the Eye.

The following are only a few, amongst the almost innumerable Cases that I have made perfect. They are inserted at the express desire of the parties:—

WM. MAIR, Garden-street, Hull, blind forty-five years of one Eye, lost from the Small Pox, was restored to Sight in six weeks so as to distinguish any object. The other Eye, the most dangerous ever man perceived was made perfect in that time, after having been an out-patient at the Dispensary for seventeen weeks. This was acknowledged by most of the medical Faculty, as well as the Inhabitants of Hull, the most wonderful cure ever performed, for he could go about the town by himself in a fortnight after having been led blind so many years.

MRS. FISHER, Short-street, Hull, blind for

EXTRAORDINARY CURES OF BLINDNESS.

MRS. BLAND, Middleton Field, Bradford, was nearly in darkness, from Amaurosis, and had been so for some years—can now see to read small print.

Mrs. WOOD, Bradford, was nearly in darkness for ten years—can see to thread the smallest needle.

JOHN FRITH, George-street, Bradford, Blacking-Hawker, was nearly in darkness for twelve years—can now see to go about the town alone, without any inconvenience.

THOMAS MALONS, of No. 146, Mill Bank, Bradford, was in total darkness for nearly three years. After having been discharged from the 31st Regiment, in consequence of blindness, he was admitted into several Hospitals, but was turned out as *incurable*. He then went under the care of one of the most eminent Oculists in London, but was declared by him to be incurable.

MISS WOODCOCK, of Peterborough, was blind for two years. Went under the care of several eminent men, but got no relief. Can now see to read the smallest print.

MRS. MERSON, Cannon-street, Old Foundry, was blind of Amaurosis, but can now see to thread the smallest needle.

MR. WOODALL, of Brigg, was also in complete darkness from Amaurosis.—He can now see to read the smallest print.

MR. GRICE, of Langtoft, near Malton, was totally blind of one eye, and the other much affected. Completely restored.

MRS. HAWKINS, wife of J. Hawkins, Paper

J. L. WARD,

Cancer Surgeon,

No. 18, Trafalgar-Street, Leeds, and No. 1, Liverpool-Street, Oldfield-Road, Manchester,

WHERE every form of Scrofula, as well as the varieties of Cancer, are treated with unerring success.

Cancer of the Tongue Cured after cutting proved ineffectual,

By J. L. WARD, 18, TRAFALGAR-STREET, Leeds, and No. 1, LIVERPOOL-STREET, Oldfield Road, Manchester.

Mr. John Wood, Gomersal, near Leeds, had an operation performed on his Tongue for Cancer, which had no other effect than the increase of this dreadful disease: he, consequently, placed himself under Mr. Ward, who has cured him effectually in five weeks, without cutting, a circumstance which he is anxious should be made known for the benefit of those who may be similarly afflicted.

Just Published, Price 7s. 6d. cloth,

HUMOUR AND PATHOS; or Essays, Tales and Sketches, by G. R. W. BAXTER, Esq., Author of "Modern Refinement," &c. &c. With Illustrations by FRANK HOWARD.

"There is a fine mixture of misanthropy and merriment throughout, and some of the delineations are excellent beyond expression. The illustrations too are of a high order."—*Conservative Journal.*

"An amusing volume; the illustrations are spirited, and the binding is among its other recommendations."—*Court Journal.*

"A very amusing volume." An amusing collection." "This book has pregnant proofs of talent." "The grave and gay will here find plentiful entertainment." "An acceptable publication." "A very pleasant collection."—*Age*, &c. &c.

London, Joseph Thomas: Sold by Simkin, Marshall and Co.

Just published, to be completed in twenty-four weekly numbers, price 3d., or in six monthly parts, price 1s., Part 1, of the

PEOPLE'S MEDICAL ADVISER,

A FAMILIAR TREATISE on the means of preserving health and the domestic treatment of diseases, particularly adapted to the use of the industrious classes;

BY MATTHEW FLETCHER,

Member of the Royal College of Surgeons, &c. Bury, Lancashire.

Published by A. Cobbett, London; and William Willis, Manchester; and sold by J. Hobson, *Northern Star Office*, Leeds, and by all Booksellers

Arrest of the Rev. J. R. Stephens.

A PUBLIC MEETING will be held on TUESDAY Evening, the 22nd of January, 1839, at Seven o'Clock, in the MAGISTRATES' OFFICE, HUDDERSFIELD, to take into consideration what is necessary to be done on account of the

ARREST OF

MR. STEPHENS.

Mr. RICHARD OASTLER has promised to attend to address the Meeting.

Admittance—Orchestra, 1s.—Saloon, 6d.—The proceeds after paying expences, to be given to Mr. Stephens.

Tickets to be had of Mr. C. Tinker, Market-Walk; Mr. L. Pitkethly, Buxton-Road; Mr. Stephen Dickenson, King-Street; Mr. Holstead, New-Street; John Stott, Woodhouse Mill; Edward Shaw, Lindley; Hannah Eastwood, Sheepridge; William Gaukroger, Paddock.

EASY EMPLOYMENT.

PERSONS having a little time to spare, are apprised that Agents continue to be appointed in London, and country Towns, by the EAST INDIA TEA COMPANY, for the sale of their celebrated Teas, (Offices, 9, Great St. Helen's, Bishopsgate-street). They are packed in leaden Canisters from an ounce to a pound (a plan found exceedingly convenient) and neither shop nor fixtures are required; the License is only 11s. per annum, Excise permits are abolished; and many during the last thirteen years have realised considerable incomes by the Agency, without 1s. let or loss. Application to be made free to CHARLES HANCOCK, Secretary.

GENERAL CONVENTION OF THE WORKING CLASSES.

NATIONAL RENT.

AT a MEETING of the COMMITTEE of DELEGATES of the GENERAL CONVENTION of the WORKING CLASSES, held at Birmingham, this 10th day of January, 1839.

BENJAMIN HADLEY, Esq.,

Churchwarden of St. Martin's Parish, Birmingham, and one of the Aldermen of the Borough of Birmingham,

IN THE CHAIR,

the following resolutions were unanimously agreed to:—

1. That it is expedient that the Delegates who have been appointed Members of the General Convention of the Industrious Classes, do meet in London, at Brown's Hotel, Palace Yard, on the 4th of February, 1839, at eleven o'clock in the forenoon precisely.

2. That the chairmen of the various public meetings throughout the kingdom, at which Delegates to the General Convention may have been appointed, be earnestly requested to forward, without delay, to Robert Kellie Douglas, *Journal Office*, Birming-

HOUSE OF RECOVERY.

AT AN EXTRAORDINARY GENERAL MEETING, held at the COURT HOUSE, on WEDNESDAY the 16th of January, at Twelve o'Clock at Noon, in order to adopt means for discharging the Debt, and placing the future operations of the Charity upon a foundation commensurate with its important objects.

The Rev. W. F. HOOK, D.D., Vicar in the Chair,

Moved by E. BAINES, Esq., M. P.
Seconded by JOHN HOWARD, Esq.

RESOLVED UNANIMOUSLY,

That, from the statement made to this meeting, it is absolutely necessary that extraordinary exertions be made to Pay the Debt, and increase the permanent Funds of the House of Recovery.

Moved by T. W. TOTTIE, Esq.
Seconded by WM. BECKETT, Esq.

RESOLVED UNANIMOUSLY,

That Application be respectfully made from the Chairman of this Meeting, to the Ministers of every Church and Chapel within the Borough, and such adjoining Places as have received Benefit from the Institution, for Congregational Collections in Aid of the Funds of the Charity.

Moved by WM. ALDAM, Esq.
Seconded by WM. WATSON, Esq.

RESOLVED UNANIMOUSLY,

That District or Ward Committees be appointed in the Borough, in order to obtain new and increased Subscriptions, together with such Donations as may be obtained, and who shall commence their operations immediately after the Congregational Collections.

Moved by JOHN HOWARD, Esq.
Seconded by THOS. HIRST, Esq.

RESOLVED UNANIMOUSLY,

That the Committee of Management of the Monthly Board be requested to carry the Resolutions of this Meeting into effect.

RESOLVED,

That the Proceedings of this Day be advertised Twice in each of the Leeds Newspapers.

W. F. HOOK, Chairman.

After the Proceedings of the Meeting, the Vicar having left the Chair, Mr. Tottie was unanimously called upon, when the Thanks of the Meeting were given to the Rev. Dr. Hook, for his urbanity and able Conduct in the Chair.

T. W. TOTTIE.

DONATIONS PAID IN THE MEETING.

	£	s.	d.		£	s.	d.
Rev. Dr. Hook	5	0	0	Henry Hall	5	0	0
Benj. Goodman	10	0	0	Mrs. Tennant	5	0	0
John Howard	5	0	0	Wm. Beckett	10	0	0
Joseph Taylor, Blenheim Terrace	5	0	0	Dr. D. Thorpe	3	0	0
T. W. Tottie	5	0	0	Edw. Wurtzburg	2	0	0
Dr. Williamson	2	0	0	Thos. Hirst	5	0	0
Miss Charlesworth	5	5	0	Christopher Beckett	10	0	0
				J. G. Uppleby	10	0	0

FULL LENGTH PORTRAIT OF THE REV. J. R. STEPHENS.

As soon as proper arrangements can be made for perfecting the work, every REGULAR Subscriber of the *Star* will be presented with a Full Length Portrait of the Christian Minister. STEPHENS will appear at Full Length, holding a Factory Child in each hand. Under one foot will be placed the "Poor Law Amendment Act," and under the other the "Factory Bill;" at the foot will be the following words:—

"These are of my flock. I am their appointed Shepherd; and whoso oppresseth them I will make war upon."

Joseph Rayner Stephens.

The above Portrait shall be worth One Guinea, and upon the day on which it appears, the *Star* shall be printed upon superfine paper, containing a BIOGRAPHY of the Glorious Champion. The Price upon that day will be to Subscribers SIXPENCE. Non-subscribers, £1. 1s. 6d. We limit the gift of the Portrait to all who shall subscribe from the first week in February, that we may know the number to order. We hope to have it ready about the time of his trial, and specimens shall be speedily placed in the hands of our several agents. To this we pledge ourselves that it shall be the most splendid present ever presented with a newspaper.

N. B. Agents are requested to keep books, with the names of Subscribers.

THE DELEGATES.

OUR strength is in our union, our power in our voice, and our success in our perseverance. For now more than four months we have had a perfect political hurricane, and the Radicals, as if their battle had been won, have been fighting among themselves. We now trust that the short interval till the meeting of all the Parliaments will be spent in sober reflection. If we do not meet in London on the 4th, without spleen and recollection of the past, far better we should not meet at all. For ourselves, we have got some crooked blows, and we have given some hard ones; but we do hereby for-

that it was wrong to get drunk. Beer, they said, made Chartists forget the wrongs they were suffering from, and so made them slack off in the fight for the Charter. At a Chartist meeting in Merthyr in June 1841 one man argued that if people gave up beer then meat would be cheaper because land used for growing barley (for making beer) could feed cattle instead!

Many Welsh Chartists were very religious. They worshipped in *Nonconformist* chapels, and read the Bible often, filling their speeches with stories from it. One Chartist said they were fighting for what 'Jesus Christ, the greatest reformer of his time' was crucified for. Sometimes Chartists attended chapel together, as a group, and one band of Merthyr Chartists even wore a special 'uniform' to do so; the men had blue flannel waistcoats and the women blue aprons. But other Chartists disliked religion, and one Chartist called ministers 'those black-coated devils who are preaching hell to their souls all day'. It is important to remember that Chartists often disagreed with each other. But all Welsh Chartists were agreed in disliking the *Anglican* Church in Wales. While the Chartists were poor, the Anglican Church was rich, and had the power to make people pay tithes to it, a sort of tax. In some places the Anglican Church often ran the only school, and Nonconformists hated having to send their children to it.

In return, Anglican clergymen hated Chartists, and the vicar of Dowlais, the Rev. Evan Jenkins, wrote a short book attacking them because their ideas were as 'opposed to the doctrines of the eternal word of God, as North is to South'. He said that men were born to be unequal and that the Devil was the first Chartist because he tried to be equal with God! Many thousands of Welsh people bought Jenkins' book, which shows us that the Charter had enemies as well as friends. What sort of people do you think would oppose the Charter?

Opposite: A front page from the Northern Star. *The 1839 Chartist petition is being collected, and the convention will meet very soon. Notice the advertisements for medicines*

A Methodist chapel at Tonyrefail, near Pontypridd, photographed about 1880

In 1840 the Chartists of Merthyr started two newspapers of their own, the 'Merthyr Advocate' and 'Udgorn Cymru' (The 'Trumpet of Wales'). 'Udgorn Cymru' was mostly in

Welsh, which reminds us that many Welsh people could not understand English at all. The two papers were published each month, and sold about 1,200 copies between them. Newspapers were expensive and several readers would share the cost. So the sale of the newspapers suggests that there were 3,000 or 4,000 Chartists in Merthyr, out of a population of about 40,000.

THE CHARTIST CONVENTION OF 1839

By the end of 1838 there were Chartist societies in nearly every town in England, Scotland and Wales. In the autumn they chose *delegates* to attend a '*Convention* of the *Industrious Classes*'. This was to be a sort of Chartist Parliament, whose job was to speak out for the people. It met in London on 4 February 1839. Fifty-four men attended. Three came from Wales – Hugh Williams, Charles Jones, and John Frost. Hugh Williams was a lawyer from Carmarthen, and Charles Jones the leader of the Chartists of Montgomeryshire (Powys). John Frost was the most famous of Welsh Chartists – a hero throughout Britain because of his part in the Newport 'rising' of 1839 and his trial afterwards. Frost was quite a rich man, like Hugh Williams and other members of the Convention; this was because poor men could not afford to spend many weeks at the Convention, away from work. Frost had a draper's shop in the High Street of Newport, and in 1836 he was chosen to be *mayor* of the town; he was also a *magistrate*.

Frost was a strong and active man, who stood out in a crowd, though he was not tall. He was handsome, though his face was marked by the scars of smallpox, a disease which many people caught in Frost's time. Frost was clever; people said that he was 'gifted by nature with far more than ordinary powers of mind'. Like many clever people, he had strong opinions. He got angry with those who disagreed with him. He was one of the leaders of the Convention, speaking a lot. Because of his work at the Convention Frost was sacked as a magistrate in March 1839.

John Frost asks for support for the People's Charter, October 1838. Chartists 'do not look for Figs from Thistles'. What does this mean?

John Frost in old age, after his return from Australia.

Members of the Convention quickly quarrelled over what Chartists ought to do when Parliament rejected the petition, as it was certain to do. Some members wanted to use only peaceful methods which did not break the law to get the Charter. They were called 'moral force' Chartists. Others talked of using force if necessary. One such man was Feargus O'Connor. You can see a picture of O'Connor on page 49. He was a tall, fat and loud-voiced Irish Chartist, who spoke fierce threats against the Whigs. He said that if peaceful methods were unsuccessful, 'then I am for war to the knife'. John Frost supported him in these tough speeches, saying that arguments would not convince the House of Commons and that force would be needed.

Some Chartists who urged the use of 'physical force' meant it. But most did not, including O'Connor and Frost. Both were excitable men, and often said more than they really intended to enthusiastic audiences who cheered fighting talk. They also thought that threats might frighten the government into surrender. But they knew that if it came to civil war the Chartists would have to fight trained soldiers with cannon and horses in pitched battles. The Chartists would lose. The government knew this too, and would not be bluffed. General Napier, commanding the army in northern England, said that he would never allow Chartists 'to charge me with their pikes, or even march ten miles [16 km], without *mauling* them with cannon and *musketry* and charging them with cavalry, when they *dispersed* to collect food'.

But many Chartists did think that force might be successful. They remembered that the Scotch Cattle were not caught for years, forgetting that attacks on blacklegs might terrify individuals but could not terrify a government. So in the spring of 1839 Chartists in many parts of Britain were secretly collecting guns and pikes. They did this in south Wales. Hopes of a revolution were encouraged there by the speeches of Henry Vincent, a 'missionary' sent from London to collect signatures to the petition.

Vincent was twenty-five years old. He was just over five feet in height. His handsome, smiling face and great skill as a speaker made him very popular in Wales. He made audiences laugh by his imitations of the Chartists' enemies, and

Henry Vincent.

then aroused their anger by fiery attacks on the unjust way masters treated workers. He called for the use of weapons. He made a typical speech in April 1839 in Newport, telling his audience that workers were not wrong if they disobeyed the law, since it was made by a Parliament that they had not helped to choose. He said that soldiers would never fire their guns on Chartists. (Vincent was very mistaken here.) He ended his speech like this: 'When the time for resistance arrives, let your cry be, "To your tents, O Israel" and then 25

TO THE

Men & Women

OF

NEWPORT.

MY FRIENDS,

You have ever found me your consistent and dauntless advocate, I have a right, therefore, to expect you are my Friends.

I am informed upon unquestionable authority that your local rulers are anxious to arrest me to night. LET THEM TAKE ME. If their conduct be legal---*well!* If illegal, they shall hereafter rue it. At the worst my detention can but be for a few days---and as Philosophy is every thing, the jails of our tyrants do not appal me.

Efforts are being made to frighten the people by calling our meetings illegal.---I never attended an illegal meeting---and there have been none of an illegal nature held within the precints of Newport, *save one held lately at Christchurch, where a man named Phillips told the mob to make their horses stand fire, and keep their powder dry!*

I am told your Magistrates are about to swear in persons as Special Constables. They have their reasons for so doing; I believe them to be bad ones, and will with your assistance, turn the mischief they may contemplate into an engine for their own legal destruction.

Meet me to night at Pentonville, where I shall do myself the honour of addressing you.

Keep the Peace I charge you!---The slightest indications of tumult on our part would afford our enemies a pretext for letting loose their Bloodhounds on us.

Keep the Peace

and laugh your enemies to scorn!

Your devoted Friend,

HENRY VINCENT.

APRIL 25th, 1839.

John Partridge, Printer, Newport

Henry Vincent defies the authorities, April 1839, just after his 'O Israel' speech. What did Phillips want?

26

with one voice, one heart and one blow perish the *privileged orders*! Death to the *aristocracy*! Up with the people and the government they have established!' (In the last sentence Vincent was referring to the Convention.)

His audience was very excited. They knew that the quotation Vincent had made from the Bible was about the revolt of the tribes of Israel against their king. Vincent was giving them a signal to encourage them to revolt against their own government.

3 The Move to Violence

LLANIDLOES RIOTS

Magistrates in South Wales and Powys were worried. The mayor of Newport wrote to the Home Secretary that 'three distinct packages of guns and muskets' had been brought to the town from Birmingham, for use by Chartists. Men at the ironworks were buying guns by weekly instalments. The Montgomeryshire (Powys) magistrates asked the Home Secretary to send soldiers. But they were needed all over Britain, and he had none to spare. Instead he sent three London policemen to help the local police catch the Chartist leaders. The three men arrived at Llanidloes on Monday 29 April 1839, and stayed overnight at the Trewythen Arms Hotel. The hotel servants spread the news of their arrival, and on Tuesday morning a Chartist called Baxter marched through the town with a 'tin horn' (a sort of trumpet) to tell people to come to a meeting at the Severn bridge, a quarter of a mile (400 m) from the inn. Meanwhile, the police arrested three Chartists and took them inside the hotel.

Someone rushed off to the meeting and told people about the arrests. Excited, the crowd rushed off to the hotel to rescue them, collecting weapons. One writer said that 'guns, *staves*, pikes, hay forks, sickles, and even spades were hastily seized by the excited and *turbulent* mob'. One old woman vowed 'that she would fight till she was knee-deep in blood, sooner than the Cockneys [the London police] should take their prisoners out of the town'. The crowd found the hotel locked against them. A magistrate was in front of the hotel, locked out by mistake. Fearing for his own safety he

28

pretended to sympathise with the crowd, shouting 'Chartists for ever' and breaking a window with his walking stick. The crowd followed his example, shattering all the glass. Eventually they burst open the front door and found the prisoners handcuffed in the kitchen. The handcuffs were sawn off. They found a policeman under a bed, and beat him up. They smashed furniture and staircases with hatchets, and tore the curtains to shreds. All the beer and wine were taken into the street; the crowd broke in the barrel ends and spilled more than they drank. After that there was no further trouble.

Meanwhile, the magistrate had slipped away from the crowd. He rode to Shrewsbury and, describing the riot, made it sound much worse than it really was. Four days after the disturbance, soldiers arrived in Llanidloes from Brecon. Thirty-two people were arrested.

The story of the riot shows that it broke out very quickly, and accidentally. There was no plot. But the government blamed the trouble on the fierce speeches that two local Chartist leaders had made some weeks before. These men were Charles Jones, the Convention member, and Thomas Powell, a Welshpool ironmonger. Neither man was in Llanidloes during the riot, which shows that they did not directly start it. The police could not find Jones, but Powell was arrested, tried and sentenced to twelve months imprisonment. Henry Vincent was arrested too, in London; he was brought back to Monmouthshire to stand trial for his 'To your tents, O Israel' speech. When he arrived at Newport 300 special constables were there to stop angry Chartists from rescuing him. At his trial Vincent was sentenced to twelve months in prison for his 'violent and *seditious* language'.

Meanwhile, Frost left the Convention to speak at monster meetings up and down Britain. As so often with Chartist leaders, his words to excited audiences influenced them to do things which were against the law. In cold blood he would not have encouraged them. When speaking to a crowd of 150,000 in Glasgow he said that if the government tried to 29

Chartists meeting at night. The magistrates have just arrived. Notice the torchlights and weapons

arrest any more Chartist leaders, 'we are determined to lay hold of some of the leading men in the country, as *hostages* for the safety of the Convention'. These words were met by 'a loud burst of cheering'. In Newport Frost suggested that the hostages should be kept down a coalmine. Words like these encouraged people to break the law. Frost tried to keep his speeches legal by saying that Chartists ought to 'hold by the law' and behave peaceably. But people believed his violent words more than his peaceful ones. The government immediately began to prosecute him without actually arresting him. The trial was not due to begin for months, but was certain to end in his conviction and imprisonment. So when Frost led the Newport rising in October he had already 'burnt his boats'. He was going to prison anyway.

THE REJECTION OF THE PETITION

Early in May the Chartists got ready to present the petition to Parliament. 1,280,000 people in Britain signed it; nearly 15,000 signed it in Merthyr Tydfil, and over 27,000 in the whole of South Wales. When the papers bearing the signatures from all over Britain were stuck together they made a roll 5 km long. It was taken across London on a decorated cart. The House of Commons voted not to agree to its demands; so the Charter was turned down.

Chartists at the Convention had to advise other Chartists on what to do next to make Parliament agree to the Charter. Many plans that people put forward were not likely to help the Charter. One was for Chartists to draw all their money out of banks to cause a financial crisis and panic the government. But Chartists were poor, and the cash they had in the bank hardly mattered. Another idea was for Chartists to refuse to drink alcohol, or to buy things from unfriendly shopkeepers. This would annoy brewers and Tory grocers, but would not bring the Charter any nearer. Eventually the leaders at the Convention decided to call for a 'sacred month', or general strike. Frost was against this idea, for good reasons. How could workers with no savings live for a month without pay? Industry was in a bad slump and employers might welcome a shut-down; Frost said that if there was a strike the Welsh *ironmasters* might close the iron- 31 works for another six months.

The Convention came to think that the sacred month would bring dreadful ruin upon thousands of poor people. It decided to recommend just a short strike of two or three days, 'in order to devote the whole of that time to solemn processions and solemn meetings'. Having made this suggestion, the Convention ended on 14 September.

By that time, many Chartists in Wales and England had decided to go much further than the Convention planned, and to try 'physical force'. This led to the march on Newport in November 1839. In South Wales the leaders of these violent Chartists were Zephaniah Williams, William Jones and William Price. Williams kept an inn in Blaina, and Jones

Pikes carried on the march to Newport, and used in evidence at the trial

one in Pontypool. Price was a doctor; his long flowing black hair and beard, which he never cut, made him seem strange, the sort of person about whom rumours easily spread.

In South Wales Chartists prepared their rising. They made pikes and cast lead bullets in moulds. Gunpowder was easy to buy, since miners used it every day in their work. Weapons were stored out of sight, in caves. There were only 500 soldiers in South Wales, but more than ten times that number of Chartists ready to fight. The plan was for the Chartists to attack all the big towns in South Wales at the same time – perhaps in the middle of the night so as to take the soldiers by surprise. Then the bridges across the river Usk were to be blown up to stop any more troops reaching Wales from England. The approach across the Bristol Channel was to be blocked by sinking ships in Newport harbour.

We cannot know all the details of the Chartist plans. Plotters do not write down their schemes, and not all the facts came out in the trials after the Newport march. When people keep plans in their heads, the stories told afterwards often disagree with each other. Yet it seems certain that risings in Yorkshire and Lancashire were planned to take place at the same time as the Welsh one. But these places were far apart and it was difficult for the leaders to keep in close touch. As we shall see, the march on Newport in fact came too early for the Yorkshire Chartists.

Frost could not make up his mind about the plans for a rising. He thought it might fail, and he was worried about violence anyway. On 3 October 500 Chartists met in Zephaniah Williams's public house in Blaina, the Royal Oak. Frost told them that other parts of Britain were not ready for rebellion, and that they ought to wait patiently for orders from him, as their leader. The Chartists yelled back at him 'Now! Tonight! Tonight!'. The meeting was stormy, and lasted till 2 o'clock in the morning. The 'hooting and yelling' of the Chartists on the way home, one newspaper wrote, 'caused so much terror in the minds of the *inhabitants* that   33 they left their beds and kept on the watch till daybreak'. Chartists wanted proper 'physical force'. One Chartist from Abersychan said:

> I will tell you, Mr Frost, the condition upon which my *lodge* will rise, and there is no other condition as far as I am concerned. The Abersychan Lodge is 1,600 strong; 1,200 of them are soldiers; the remaining 400 have never handled arms, but we can turn them into fighting men in no time. I have come to tell you that we shall not rise until you give us a list of those we have to remove – to kill.

Early in October Frost agreed to join the risings but was frightened at the thought of bloodshed. On 27 October he talked over the plans for the rising with Dr Price. 'What', said Frost, 'do you want us to kill the soldiers – kill a thousand of them in one night?' 'Yes', Price answered, 'a hundred thousand if it is necessary'. Frost then said 'I cannot do it; I cannot do it'. He 'wept like a child and talked of heaven and hell'. Later, when he was in prison, Frost said that he knew he was not the right man to lead the rising, 'for the moment I saw blood flow I became terrified and fled, but what was I to do?' Frost felt that he had to stay loyal to other Chartists. They would have suspected him of giving up his beliefs if he had backed out of the rising. What would you have done if you had been Frost?

Frost knew that the government had learnt about the plans through its spies, and that the soldiers would be ready for the Chartist attack. Special constables would be recruited to help them. Frost therefore thought that there were not enough Chartists to capture every town at once. So he persuaded the other leaders that the Chartist 'brigades' should attack Newport first and then march on the other towns. Frost knew that the rising would be even harder for the Chartists, now that they could not surprise the soldiers. Do you think that the Chartists ought to have called the rising off?

The march on Newport was fixed for the night of Sunday 3 November. The Welsh and English Chartists knew of each others' plans, sending messengers by roundabout ways because they did not dare to use the post. Late in October the Yorkshire Chartists realised that they would not be ready by early November, and sent a messenger to Frost to ask him to delay the Welsh rising for ten days. He saw Frost in Blackwood on 2 November. Frost told him that it was too late to postpone the rising, and that he 'might as well blow his own brains out as to try to oppose them or shrink back'. The messenger left to return to Yorkshire at 9.00 pm. Frost burnt letters he did not want the police to find if he was arrested. Next day, the Chartists marched on Newport.

THE ATTACK ON NEWPORT, NOVEMBER 1839

Chartists gathered in the towns to the north of Newport on Saturday and Sunday, 2 and 3 November. Guns and pikes were collected from their secret stores. Some men, frightened of bloodshed or disliking Chartism, were forced to join the march.

> A band of 40 or 50 Chartists, armed with pikes, guns and other mortal weapons, march to a house, and if the door is not instantly opened to them they at once attack and demolish it. They then enter the house in a body, and demand that the master and every other man on the premises join their ranks, stating that no harm shall come to the women or children, as they are sworn not to injure them. If the master refuses he is then seized and dragged forth, placed in the centre of the band, and a file of men behind him with presented pikes, and thus marched off.

Magistrates and police watched helplessly. Rich people were afraid for their lives. The ironmaster Charles Lloyd Harford saw on Sunday that the furnaces had been blown out in his ironworks at Sirhowy and that 'there were already assembled large masses of miners etc (and of his own men some thousands) armed, ammunitioned, and ready for 35 action'. With his family and servants Harford left for safety in Cheltenham on Sunday evening. At Tredegar, the manager of the bank feared that Chartists might seize its cash, and so he took it from the safe and carried it to Abergavenny, away from the danger. Hundreds of people fled to Abergavenny early in November.

In the evening of Sunday 3 November Chartists started their march to Newport, from Blackwood, Pontypool and the towns at the Heads of the Valleys. They walked in small groups, carrying pikes and guns, with some bread and cheese in their pockets. They marched in pitch darkness, and in pouring rain, along tracks that were often very hard to follow.

South Wales in Chartist times

Chartists were not trained to march like soldiers, and the columns struggled along miles of road. Wet through, some Chartists stopped on the way, forcing public houses to open up in the middle of the night and let them in to get dry.

They were all supposed to meet outside Newport. The first Chartists, from Blackwood and Argoed, reached Risca (near Newport) about midnight. When they met they cheered and fired their guns, so giving a warning to soldiers on patrol from Newport.

Frost and the Chartists who had arrived at Risca should have attacked Newport right away. Instead, worried as ever, he decided to wait for the others to join them. So Chartists stayed at Risca for up to six hours, getting wetter. Meanwhile, the magistrates in Newport had time to prepare for the attack.

When dawn broke there were about 5,000 Chartists waiting to attack. A man watching the columns wrote later about the

> 'hosts of drenched, *begrimed*, fatigued, and many apparently frightened men, who lined the road for a considerable distance . . . This party was the section immediately under Mr Frost's command, waiting for the other divisions to join them, and consisted of several thousands of men, nearly all armed, some with pikes, fixed on well-made handles or shafts, some more roughly made; crude spears, formed of rod iron sharpened at one end, and turned into a loop at the other as a handle; guns, muskets, pistols, coal mandrills (a sharp double-pointed pick-axe used in cutting coals), clubs, *scythes*, *crow-bars*; and in fact, any and every thing that they could lay their hands on.'

He wrote that the Chartists had the oddest jumble of weapons ever brought 'to compete with disciplined and well-armed forces. It was folly; it was frenzy; it was sheer insanity; downright madness!'

At about 7 o'clock the Chartists marched off towards

Newport, in columns with pikemen in the centre and gunmen at the side. Outside the town Frost asked some boys where the soldiers were. They replied that some had gone to the Westgate Hotel in the centre of the town. 'We want the Westgate', a Chartist shouted, to which another replied 'I want a waistcoat, for mine is damned wet'. The Chartists marched into Newport down Stow Hill.

There were only seventy soldiers in the town, from the 45th Regiment. The magistrates learned on Sunday evening that the Chartists were approaching. Frightened, they sent a messenger to Bristol, by way of Beachley Ferry, to ask for more troops. Some were sent across by steamboat. It stuck on a *sandbank*, and the extra soldiers did not reach Newport till Tuesday morning. Meanwhile, on Sunday evening the Newport magistrates recruited 500 *special constables*, who arrested many local Chartists and guarded some of them in the Westgate Hotel.

On Monday morning the mayor ordered thirty soldiers to defend the Westgate Hotel. They arrived at 8.30, and were placed in a room at the front overlooking Commercial Street. They could not be seen from the street because there were shutters over the windows.

The first Chartists arrived in front of the Westgate about 9.20. They were led by John Rees, a stonemason from Tredegar, who had fought in Texas against the Mexicans. The Chartists shouted to some constables in the doorway 'Give us up the prisoners'. A constable shouted 'No, never'. Chartists rushed into the hall of the inn. As constables and Chartists scuffled inside the hall, someone opened fire – we don't know who. In the room where the soldiers were, bullets came through the glass above the shutters, and went into the ceiling. The soldiers were ordered to load their guns. The mayor and Lieutenant Gray took the shutters down. A bullet hit the mayor in the hip. Gray immediately ordered his men

Opposite: Outside the Westgate Hotel, Newport, 9.30 am, 4 November 1839. There were no children in the street at the time. Why has the artist added them?

WESTGATE HOTEL

Drawn & Engraved by John Wood Jun.r Bristol. THE CHARTIST ATTACK AT NEWPORT Nov.r 4th 1839.

to fire. They fired into the street for half a minute and then into the hall of the inn for ten minutes. The inn was filled with smoke and the noise was very great. In the confusion, the mayor was nearly shot by a soldier.

When the soldiers fired, the Chartists in Commercial Street retreated, except for a man with a wooden leg who stayed to shoot three times at the inn. Inside the inn the Chartists fought on in the noise and smoke for ten minutes more, until they too had to withdraw. Twenty-two Chartists were killed. Among them was George Shell, aged nineteen. This is a letter he had written the previous evening:

Dear Parents,

I hope this will find you well, as I am myself at present. I shall this night be *engaged* in a struggle for freedom, and should it please God to spare my life, I shall see you soon; but if not, grieve not for me. I shall fall in a noble cause. My tools are at Mr Cecil's, and likewise my clothes.

What sort of man do you think George Shell was?

Only 200 or 300 Chartists took part in the attack. After it some Chartists panicked and fled to the hills, but there were still many armed Chartists in the town or marching towards it. The Chartists did not leave Newport till the afternoon, and some people expected another attack on Monday night. For some days Chartists in South Wales thought of continuing the fight. On Tuesday 5 November, for example, the Rhondda and Pontypridd men talked of attacking Cardiff, where the mayor recruited many special constables, placed cannon on the roads leading to the city, and arranged to ring the church bells if the Chartists marched.

They didn't. The collapse of the Newport attack made Chartists fearful. 'Go home and be quiet', the Merthyr Chartists were told in the evening of 5 November; 'our friends at

Opposite: A close-up view of the attack on the Westgate Hotel

Newport have jumped over the hedge too soon'. More soldiers were marching from Winchester towards South Wales, and cannon were being moved in by the Great Western Railway. A revolution was getting harder.

Immediately after the Newport fighting Frost was seen just outside the town, crying into a handkerchief. He hid in a coal waggon, and at night came back into Newport. He was arrested at a neighbour's. William Jones was captured in a wood near Crumlin a week later.

Zephaniah Williams was caught three weeks after the rising in a ship about to sail to Portugal. Other leading Chartists escaped; some of them reached Liverpool and sailed for America. Dr William Price disappeared just before the march. Perhaps he guessed that it would end in disaster. He reappeared in Paris, where he was safe from arrest by British police.

Why did the rising fail? The Chartists made bad mistakes. They should have captured or destroyed the bridges over the Usk. At Newport they should have surprised the soldiers by attacking in the middle of the night. In the morning of 4 November it might have been better to capture the rest of the town before attacking the inn. In any case could the rising ever have succeeded in the long run? Here the answer is surely 'No', even if there had been risings in England too. The army was too strong, and more people in Britain were against the Chartists than on their side. The South Wales rising was a gamble that was sure to be lost.

But what do you think? Could it have succeeded? Would it have been good for Wales and for Britain if it had been successful?

THE TRIAL

The government put Frost, Williams, William Jones and nine other men on trial for treason. This was the crime of using force, or even planning to use force, to overthrow the government or to compel it to do something against its will. Death was the penalty for people found guilty. Before the trial Chartists collected money to pay lawyers to defend the twelve men in court; for example the Chartists of Aberdare gave £45. Feargus O'Connor raised the price of his newspaper, the 'Northern Star', by 1*d*. (½p) a copy to get money for the defence.

The trial began in Monmouth on 31 December. The prisoners were brought into court handcuffed and chained together in groups of six, to prevent an escape. Police were brought down from London to keep order; there were ten policemen in court.

The defence lawyers tried to show that the violence had been accidental and that the Chartists had planned only a big demonstration. The *prosecution* pointed out that nobody ever planned a demonstration at night, when people would not see it. They also pointed out that marching with weapons was itself treason, and so was the attack on the Westgate Inn. Eight men were found guilty, though the case against four others was dropped because of lack of evidence. Five men were sentenced to be *transported*, but Frost, Jones and Williams were sentenced to death.

For three weeks these three men were in the *condemned cell*, and able to hear the carpenter making the gallows on which they were to be hanged. But many people pleaded for mercy, and the government decided to reduce the penalty to transportation for life, to Tasmania in Australia. Frost and the others were awakened in the middle of the night, told they had been *reprieved*, and were taken to Chepstow in handcuffs and chains, and guarded by six policemen and twenty-four cavalrymen; the government feared that an attempt night be made to rescue them. At four o'clock in the morning they sailed to Portsmouth. Soon they were on their way to Tasmania; they were not allowed to see their families before leaving.

4 Slump, Strike and the Land Plan

1842: SLUMP AND STRIKE

Newport showed that Chartists had been determined and thought they would succeed. It also showed that they were weak. Their demonstration did not make the government afraid, and was scattered by a few soldiers.

1842 showed again that Chartists had little power. The slump returned, worse than ever. In Sheffield men and women scrabbled in the fields for potatoes and harnessed themselves to ploughs, like horses, to dig them up. In Lancashire unemployed weavers boiled nettles for food. In South Wales one employer wrote, 'from the low wages men are earning and many not being able to get employ it is not to be wondered at the men being ready to listen to anything that they may tell them would lessen their distress'. You can see why hungry and desperate people turned again to the Charter hoping to improve their lives.

In April another Chartist Convention met in a public house near Fleet Street in London, to draw up another petition for Parliament. A weaver called Morgan Williams from Merthyr Tydfil was a representative from South Wales, and there were twenty-four from other parts of Britain. The petition mentioned the Six Points of course, and also the cruelty of the Poor Law, low wages and long hours of work. The petition was signed by over 3,300,000 people, 36,000 of them in Merthyr and other towns nearby. There were so

Opposite: Carrying the Chartist petition to Parliament, 1842. Notice the children carrying hoops.

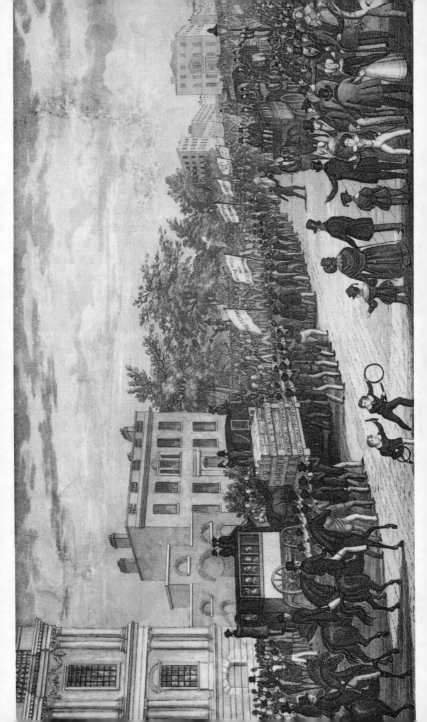

many sheets of paper that fifty men had to carry a bundle each to Parliament. With their supporters they made a procession 3 km long. But Members of Parliament took no notice of the fact that so many people supported the petition. They turned it down by 287 votes to 49. MPs said that if votes and power were given to poor people they would use them to share wealth more equally. This was true, and most MPs did not want it. The Convention broke up. Chartist leaders did not know what they could do next.

In June 1842 strikes started in the Midlands and spread to Lancashire and Yorkshire quickly. In August the collieries and ironworks around Merthyr began to strike. You can read about the problems in Merthyr in another Then and There book 'Merthyr Iron and Merthyr Riots'. Many of the strikers were Chartists and looked to the Six Points to better their lives. But it was very hard for the strikers to succeed. Employers were not very bothered for they had already stored up more coal and iron than they could sell. Many workers felt that striking was hopeless, and some strikers were soon waiting for a chance to go back to work. On 20 August the ironmaster Crawshay asked his striking workmen to return to his ironworks, and sent a man ringing a bell round Merthyr to spread the message. The strikers returned to work.

But many Chartists were given the sack for the part they had played in the strike. One of them, William Taylor, a miner, said that 'there are many of us picked out and turned off from our employment which is a great loss to us'. But, he said, 'we shall not be many days before we shall see all those Tyrannical under our feet and the Charter the law of the Land'. Many Welsh Chartists felt that since petitioning and striking had been failures, force was the only means left. William Miles, a miner, said in October that 'the last argument with a King was a Cannon and now when you see that moral force is no good, that ought to be your last argument.

Opposite: High Street Merthyr Tydfil, 1840. Notice the man ringing a handbill, on the left

46

Everyone ought to learn how to use a gun and everyone ought to have one in his possession, for government would never be afraid until they saw the people buying arms.' In this piece, 'the last argument with a King was a Cannon' refers to the civil war of 1642–48.

In the autumn of 1842 Chartist meetings were too big for public houses and hundreds of men gathered on the hillsides instead. Many Welsh Chartists were paying a regular amount each week to buy arms. Arms clubs were started at the Travellers and Old Angel public houses in Merthyr. Buying weapons helped Chartists to believe that they were doing something useful, but Newport had shown that force would most probably fail disastrously. The government knew all about the weapons from spies that got into Chartist meetings. An armed rebellion by Chartists would not be a surprise, and trained soldiers could beat ordinary people in a battle. In hilly countryside armed Chartists might be a nuisance as *guerrilla fighters*, but they could not overthrow the government by doing that. By 1844 Welsh Chartists had realised that force could not succeed. They stopped their arms clubs, and turned to a new idea to make their lives happier – the Chartist Land Plan.

THE LAND PLAN

The Land Plan was the idea of Feargus O'Connor, the best-known of all Chartists. He was tall man with red hair who stood out in a crowd. His speeches interested and persuaded huge Chartist audiences. It was about 1843 when O'Connor became very excited about his ideas for settling many thousands of poor Chartists on small farms. They would grow food and live in comfort. They would be their own masters too.

O'Connor started a company for his plan. It was called the National Land Company. Chartists could join it by paying as little as 1s (5p) a week; so it was open even to the very poor. Seventy thousand Chartists in Britain joined the

Feargus O'Connor in 1848

scheme, more people than actually paid money for any other Chartist activity. The money was used to buy five large blocks of land before the scheme ended about 1850. (These 49 five places are marked on the map on p 6.) The land was divided into plots where cottages were built for the settlers. There were only about 300 cottages and the lucky settlers were chosen by a 'lucky dip'.

Out of about 300 branches of the National Land Company in Britain, about 25 were in Wales. Of these, Merthyr had the most people and the most members, in three branches. Other large towns with mines or industries also had branches – places like Cardiff, Swansea and Ebbw Vale (see map on p. 36). But members also came from little places like Mold and Montgomery where there was no industry. This was because other people besides miners and factory workers were also drawn by O'Connor's dream. Shopkeepers and farm labourers liked the idea of leading healthy and well-fed lives in the open air, and being the boss of a small farm. O'Connor's plan was brilliant because it appealed to so many people, and promised them happiness without their having to get the People's Charter first.

O'Connor never worked out his plan properly. The 70,000 members thought they were all going to get plots soon. O'Connor planned to do this by using the rents from the earlier settlements to buy more land. But it would have taken 150 years to settle all the members in this way. Chartists began to think that perhaps the plan was hopeless and stopped paying money into it. After the first five settlements, there were no more.

The Land Plan was a disappointment. The plots, of 4 acres (1.6 hectares) each, were usually too small to give the settlers a proper living. They had to have other jobs as well.

Nowadays the cottages have often been extended to make larger houses, and the plots sell for very large amounts. Crops are not grown on them, and they are often just large gardens. Britain has changed a great deal since Chartist times.

A Chartist picture of O'Connorville, the settlement near London, 1845. It tries to show the comfort and happiness of the settlers' lives

51

5 The Final Outcome

WHAT HAPPENED TO THE CHARTISTS

The petition of 1848, which started out from Snig's End in a cart made nearby, was the last large Chartist action. O'Connor planned to have a huge Chartist meeting in London on 10 April, and carry the petition in a procession to the House of Commons. The meeting was held, but the procession was banned by the government. O'Connor, already suffering from mental illness, was frightened underneath his shouts and boasting. He did not try to argue with the police, but took the petition to Parliament in three *cabs*. The crowds walked home in the pouring rain. Parliament refused this petition like the others.

But after 1848 life got better in Britain for many people. The dreadful slumps of the 1840s ended. In the 1850s prices dropped, and people had more to eat. Many were still very poor by our standards, but as the 'Northern Star' complained, 'as soon as they got employment they totally forgot their political duties'.

The 1850s and 1860s were boom years for miners and iron-workers in South Wales. The building of railways all over the world led to a demand for iron rails, which Wales met by making more iron. This meant that more coal was needed too.

In Wales just a small band of men were left 'to keep the Chartist flag flying' (as one of them put it). They kept hopeful by dreaming of a 'great and glorious' movement which would end in the freeing of the 'crushed and degraded' workers. But no such revolution took place. Instead, there were slow small victories. One Chartist, Morgan Williams, helped to start Merthyr Tydfil library; education was always something that Chartists were enthusiastic about. Others were elected to Boards of Guardians and fought for a more kindly Poor Law.

A very late victory for Chartist ideas came in 1867 when another Reform Bill gave the vote to many working men (still not women, though). The number of voters in Merthyr Tydfil, for example, went up from 1,400 to 14,600. At the next election old Chartists worked for a Radical candidate, Henry Richard, and the new voters elected him to Parliament – the first MP to be chosen in Wales by working people.

People stopped calling themselves Chartists. But they still worked for the Six Points and for the power for ordinary people that the Six Points would lead to. One by one, five of the Six Points were won, the last of the five being gained in 1918 – the vote for all men over 21. Ten years later all women over 21 were given the vote too – something that some Chartists would have liked, and others wouldn't.

The sixth point – Annual Parliaments – hasn't been won. Nobody really wants them now. They would mean the fuss of elections every year, and perhaps frequent changes of government which might mean that nothing would be done properly.

THE FATE OF THE NEWPORT THREE

After a voyage of four months Frost, Williams and Jones reached the convict settlement at Port Arthur, Tasmania. All three were at first treated quite lightly, though Frost and Williams were afterwards handled very harshly.

Jones was made a warder and teacher at the prison for transported boys. Soon he was allowed to leave the settlement and to work where he chose on the island. He became a coachman, then one job after another – a watchmaker, an actor and an innkeeper. After years of poverty and illness he died in 1873.

On arriving at Port Arthur, Williams was put to his old 53

PRICE ONE SHILLING

Port Arthur

VAN DIEMEN'S LAND

PUBLISHED
BY
J·W·BEATTIE
HOBART.

trade; he was made a foreman in a coalmine, where convicts were the miners. He tried to escape, but after four days in the bush gave himself up. He was then given the very severe punishments which were kept for convicts who broke the rules, and which made the British prisons in Australia the most cruel and savage ones in the world. Williams was sentenced to two years' hard labour in chains. He broke up stones with a large hammer, while chained to two murderers. He spent sixteen weeks in total silence in an unlit cell measuring six feet by four (1.8 by 1.2 m). After his time in the cells Williams was moved to huts, where thousands of *lice* crawled in the blankets.

Afterwards his life became easier, and in 1853 he was given a pardon. He turned to coalmining for himself, and made a lot of money at it. In 1855 he found the Mersey coal seam, two feet (0.6 m) thick, covering 2,000 acres (800 hectares), and only thirty-five feet (11 m) below the ground. It proved to be the best seam in Australia and New Zealand; soon Williams was exporting his coal outside Tasmania. Meanwhile, Williams's wife was keeping an inn in Caerphilly. The voyage between Britain and Australia was too long and unpleasant for her or Williams to make when they were old. Williams died in 1874, not having seen his family since the 'mad enterprise', as he called it, thirty-five years before.

When Frost arrived in Tasmania in 1840 he was at first given a quite easy job in the office of the convict settlement's commander. Here he saw the immense cruelty with which convicts were punished – something he remembered bitterly for the rest of his life; Frost was an unselfish man who hated the sufferings of other people as much as his own. Frost saw so many convicts flogged, one after another, that the ground beneath the *triangle* they were tied to was soaked with blood.

Frost was not long in the office. In a letter home he criticised the Home Secretary, Lord John Russell, an old enemy from Chartist days. Frost's words were published; Russell decided he must be punished. Frost was sentenced to two years' hard labour. At fifty-seven he was given the job of breaking stones. He was pardoned in 1854 and given permission to live anywhere but in Britain.

He travelled to the United States, and in 1856 was told that he might return home. He arrived home in July, aged seventy. A crowd of 1,000 gave him a hero's welcome in Newport. Men drew him through the streets in a carriage decorated with flowers. Outside the Westgate Hotel they stopped for a few minutes while the crowd cheered. From a window nearby Frost spoke to the crowd, telling them that he hadn't changed his ideas in seventeen years. He still wished to see the Charter made law.

Frost was now seventy years old and too old to be able to

Convicts breaking stones in Australia, 1847

carry out his hope of returning to active work for radical political reform. For some time he gave lectures on the Newport rising and the wickedness of the convict system, but soon he gave these up. He lived on till 1877, dying at the age of ninety-two. His death surprised people; they had not known he was still alive. Like the Chartist movement itself, he was half-forgotten. But his ideas survived: most of the things the Chartists wanted were finally gained by the people.

How do we know?

We are lucky in being able to read many of the Chartists' own memories. So when we are trying to find out about John Frost's part in the events of this time, we can go straight to his own story, in writings such as *The Horrors of Convict Life* (1856).

We get a different point of view in the writings of people who disliked Chartism, such as Barnabas Brough, a brewer from Pontypool; his account of the march on Newport is quoted on p 37.

Newspapers give many details of events. The Chartists published one, the 'Northern Star'; copies of this may be found in large libraries. You should be able to see copies of other newspapers from Chartist times in your local library.

Books written a long time after the Chartists also give us information: for example, *Chartism and the Chartists* by David Jones (1975), and *Chartist Studies* edited by Asa Briggs (1959), which has a chapter on Chartism in Wales. You can read about the Newport rising in *South Wales and the Rising of 1839* by Ivor Wilks (1984), and *The Last Rising: the Newport Insurrection of 1839* by David J.V. Jones (1985). The lives of Chartist leaders are described in *Chartist Portraits* by G.D.H. Cole (1941) and *John Frost* by David Williams (1939)

Things to do

1. Hold a class discussion on how the lives of poor people today have changed since Chartist times.
2. Imagine that you have taken part in the march on Newport. Write your diary of the night's events.
3. Have you ever met people like John Frost in real life? If so, describe them.
4. Imagine that you are delegates to the 1839 Convention, and hold a class discussion on what should be done to make the Charter law.
5. Visit your reference library and see if it has any copies of local newspapers from either the summer of 1839 or August 1842. Read accounts of Chartist meetings and write about them.
6. Write the diary of a magistrate, soldier or policeman in Newport in November 1839.
7. Find a picture of a street in your town in the 1840s and describe how it has changed today.
8. Imagine that you are one of the Newport convicts transported to Tasmania. Write your diary for a week in the prison.
9. Write and act one of these scenes:
   (a) A meal in a workhouse. Charles Dickens' novel, 'Oliver Twist', will help you with this.
   (b) A Chartist dinner in honour of Henry Vincent.
10. Make a book with descriptions and pictures of things in the 1840s (clothes, food, houses) on one side and accounts and pictures of corresponding things today opposite. Volume 3 of 'Everyday Things in England', by C.H.B. and M. Quennell (Batsford), will help you with the 1840s.
11. Visit Newport and look at John Frost Square and the wall-picture of the Chartists. Draw another wall-picture with more scenes from Chartist history.

Glossary

Anglican Church, the Church of England, or Church of Wales
aristocracy, small group of rich and powerful landowners
ballot, voting by marking a choice on a slip of paper
begrimed, covered with dust or dirt
blacklegs, people who work when their fellow workers are
   on strike
boom, time when trade is good and more people are employed
cabs, horse-drawn carriages hired like taxis
Chartists, people who worked for the People's Charter
to commit, here means to accuse someone of a crime
condemned cell, room in prison occupied by those about to be
   hanged
constituencies, areas electing members to Parliament
Convention, meeting to decide important questions
crow-bars, iron bars used as levers
delegates, people chosen to give the opinions of a group at a
   meeting
depression, here means time when trade is going down and
   people are losing their jobs
to discharge, to set free
to disperse, to scatter
dresser, large wooden cupboard with open shelves on top
to engage, here means to take part in
to emancipate, to free
frenzy, wildness
guardians, here means persons elected to run the Poor Law in an
   area
guerrilla fighters, fighters who hide in wild country and attack their
   enemies in small groups
hostages, people kept prisoner by people who wish to force their
   friends to do something those people want

Industrious Classes, working classes

inhabitants, people living in a town or district

ironmaster, owner of an ironworks

lice, tiny crawling insects that spread disease

lodge, here means a local group of Chartists

magistrate, local judge, usually dealing with less serious crimes

mauling, handling with violence

mayor, elected leader of a town

musketry, guns, the size and shape of rifles

Nonconformists, Protestant people who will not go to the Anglican Church – Baptists, Congregationalists, Methodists, etc. They worship in Chapels

paupers, people getting poor relief

People's Charter, paper with a list of the people's demands

Poor Law, law which said how much help should be given to the poor

privileged orders, people with far more money and power than most

prosecution, in a trial, the lawyers trying to prove the guilt of the persons accused

publicans, owners or managers of public houses

Radicals, people wanting large changes in society

recommendation, here means advice

to reprieve, to release someone from the sentence of a law court

sandbank, long pile of sand in river or harbour, a danger to ships

scythes, large curved blades used for cutting grass

seditious, describes anything likely to lead people to riot or rebel

slump, time when trade is bad and there are many people unemployed

special constable, temporary policeman

staves, sticks

ticket of leave, permission for convicts to live outside the prison

Tories, nineteenth-century political party usually supporting people with property

tram-roads, early railways for horse-drawn wagons

transported, taken to a prison overseas (usually Australia)

triangle, here means a large wooden structure to which men are strapped to be flogged

turbulent, noisy

turnpike gate, payment place on a road that you pay to travel on

tyrannical, using cruelty to force people to obey you

Whigs, nineteenth-century political party opposed to the Tories,
but, like them, usually supporting people with property

workhouse, prison-like home for people receiving poor relief

Index

Acknowledgements

The author wishes to thank the friends who have assisted him when writing this book, and in particular Dr Angela John for very helpful advice and the loan of her unpublished University of Wales thesis 'The Chartists of Industrial South Wales 1840–1868' (1970), and Jill Waterhouse for advice on Australian illustrations.

Small extracts taken from: Asa Briggs, *Chartist Studies*, Macmillan 1959, pages 4, 17; David Jones, *Before Rebecca*, Allen Lane 1973, page 9; O.R. Ashton, 'Chartism in Mid–Wales', *Montgomeryshire Collections* 62, Part 1, 1971, page 11; Peter Searby, 'Chartists and Freemen in Coventry', *Social History*, 6, Methuen 1977, page 12; D. Williams, *The Rebecca Riots*, University of Wales Press 1955, page 13; David Jones, 'Chartism in Welsh Communities', *Welsh History Review* 6, University of Wales Press 1972–3, page 19; Angela John, 'The Chartists of Industrial South Wales 1840–68' University of Wales (unpublished MA thesis 1970), pages 19, 52; David Williams, *John Frost: A Study in Chartism*, University of Wales Press 1939, pages 21, 25–7, 33–4, 38, 41; J.T. Ward, *Chartism*, Batsford 1973, page 24; Dorothy Thompson, *The Early Chartists*, Macmillan 1971, pages 28, 37; R.G. Gammage, *History of the Chartist Movement*, reprinted by Merlin Press 1969, pages 30–1, 32; Ivor Wilks, *South Wales and the Rioting of 1939*, Croom Helm 1984, page 35; W. Morgan, 'Chartism and Industrial South Wales in 1842', *National Library of Wales Journal* x, 1957–8, page 44; David Jones, 'Chartism at Merthyr', *Bulletin Board Celtic Studies*, 24, 1972, pages 46–8.

We are grateful to the following for permission to reproduce photographs: BBC Hulton Picture Library, pages 14, 56–7; Cambridge University Library, page 54; Mary Evans Picture Library, page 8; Guildhall Library, page 45; Mrs Alice Mary Hadfield, page 51; Mansell Collection, pages 25, 30, 49; Merthyr Tydfil Central Library, page 47; National Library of Wales, Cardiff, page 39; Newport Central Library, pages 22, 40; Newport Museum and Art Gallery, pages 23, 26, 32; Welsh Folk Museum, pages 10, 20.

We are grateful to Newport Central Library and The Starling Press for permission to adapt the map on page 36 from *The Chartist Movement in Monmouthshire* by James Davies, 1981.

Cover: Chartist attack on the Westgate Hotel, Newport 1839; National Library of Wales.